Because God is good!

Foundations

Foundations

Intro
Prayer
The why
Instructions
My story
Day 1: The Fall
Day 2: Repentance
Day 3: Forgiveness
Day 4: Baptism
Day 5: Mercy
Day 6: Grace
Day 7: Faith
Day 8: Holy Spirit
Day 9: Spiritual gifts
Day 10: Fruit of the Spirit
Day 11: God is Love
Day 12: Trinity
Day 13: Prayer
Day 14: Ask and Receive
Day 15: Community
Day 16: Fellowship
Day 17: Put God First
Day 18: Put off the Old
Day 19: Seek Wisdom and Knowledge
Day 20: Satan's Plan
Day 21: Spiritual Warfare
Day 22: Untruths
Day 23: Open your Bibles
Day 24: Rejoice
Day 25: Fear Not
Day 26: Anxiety
Day 27: Give Thanks
Day 28: Light and Salt
Day 29: Trust
Day 30: The Great Commission

Foundations

All biblical scriptures referenced or quoted are from the English Standard Version.

Intro

When God calls you to do something…. well…. you better do it or He will put you in a position where you have nothing to do but what He's called you to do. In the summer of 2019, I felt the Lord put on my heart to write a devotional book and so I began. I worked hard and was in prayer and quiet time; seeking and knocking and the first 10 devotions came quick and easy. Ha! How funny to think 10 pages was easy? Then the distractions came in; work, life, kids and 6 months later I find myself unemployed with tons of time on my hands seeking God's will for my days. Again, the call comes, "write my devotional and call in Foundations." Ok Lord, here you go, it's for Your Glory, Your Kingdom and may it bless all those who read it.

Let's pray

Father God, you are the Wonderful and Almighty God! Your love knows no boundaries. You love us so much that you are constantly calling out to us to come back to you. I thank you for each and every person who opens this devotional. I pray the words on the pages will penetrate their heads, flow to their hearts and they will come face to face with YOU! I pray they will receive your love and grow and not fight the process. I ask that their circumstances will allow them time to read it and truly absorb who you are. Then, Father, please show them who you created them to be. Protect them from the lies of the enemy that says they are not enough or never going to be who You want them to be. Protect them from condemnation, shame and all negativity as

Foundations

they grow. I pray their families will be touched and that generations will be changed forever through this devotional. I pray for wisdom and knowledge into the mysteries of You that will be revealed to those who read it. I pray they will grow in love, grace and mercy. Thank you for your Word, that it is meaningful and important to this day! I thank you Lord for the gift of this calling. I pray my words will be Your words and everything will come directly from You. I pray my flesh will be quieted and only the spirit and your righteousness will flow through me. I thank you Lord in advance for this creation! May it also be a blessing to me and my family as we step into being the people You called us to be. Amen.

The why

The purpose of this devotional book is to spend time with the Lord. The only way to get to know someone is by spending time with them. God loves you! He's got great plans for your life that only you are able to fulfill and the only way to know those plans are to know HIM! You are beautiful and wonderfully made in His image and He wants to be reconciled back into closer relationship with YOU (Psalm 139:14)!! Do you have a relationship with the Lord? I grew up in the church and still missed out on so many foundational concepts of Christianity found in the scriptures. I was a lukewarm Christian. I wasn't taught or mentored into a flourishing relationship with God. I never knew the power of the Holy Spirit or who He was and how He was related to Jesus and God. Sure, my church did a great job letting me know God loved me and who He was but there was truly no relationship. Reconciliation, restoration and relationship are truly what God wants with you and everyone!!

Foundations

Throughout my journey into closer relationship with God, I learned many amazing things: wisdom and knowledge into scriptures, what the Trinity is and who God really is and who He made me to be. I learned what faith looks like, how to pray for myself and others and how to include thanksgiving in my worship. THESE are so super important! These are foundational concepts that are crucial to growing in Christ; so valuable that God wants me to share them with you! The purpose is to build you up closer to Him for the glory and increase to the Kingdom.

Instructions

I want you to take the next 30 days and really lean into the Lord. He's been calling you back into relationship with Him for a long time and I think now is a better time than ever to say YES! Each day read the devotion, then the scriptures associated with the message and of course, answers the questions! All scripture is from God so if you ever wonder what God says about something, open your Bible! Yes, I tend to write with a lot of exclamations but I'm passionate about what God says and who He is. Plus, it's important! It's building a solid foundation into a loving and mature relationship with our Savior. Hence, FOUNDations!

I also want to encourage you to read the full chapter of the scriptures given. This is something I began doing a while back as it really helps set up a better picture of what is happening. Sometimes scriptures are given completely out of context so it's good to have the bigger picture of what is going on that causes the Lord to say what He says and why. A bonus to you if you do that is you learn more about the Bible than a single verse. It's a win, win!

Foundations

Thank you, Jesus, for calling me to share these key foundational concepts to help people grow into a loving relationship with You!

I wanted to share my testimony and do it in such a way that you know exactly who is writing this devotional. I'm not a seminary graduate, I don't have 6 degrees behind my name. I am a married woman with 2 teenage sons living in Bend, Oregon and I love the Lord! I know Him and He knows me. I am a God honoring woman who grew up in the church yet missed it! My husband and I have been through the most challenging of times to be where we are now spiritually and I blame that (in a good way) on the Lord. See, many are called but few are chosen. I say that not to be boastful but to let you know that the Lord sought us out and it's been the most beautiful holy roller coaster ride of our lives. No one ever said it would be easy. God has reconciled me to Him and He's healed my broken heart and for that I am eternally humbled and grateful.

<u>My story</u>

As mentioned, I grew up in the church. My beautiful mother was the music minister and one of the founding members of our small Disciples of Christ Christian church in Tucson, Arizona. We went to church every Sunday growing up and my family alone, made up half of the congregation. At the age of 10, I learned from my mom that my dad had a drug and alcohol problem and was no longer taking care of us. I had no idea!! I was a kid, of course I didn't know the struggles of my parents. We moved 8 times in 6 years and were eating dinner out each night. Unbeknownst to me, my dad quit giving my mom money for groceries and we were kicked out of all of those houses because of non-payment. Again, I repeat, I had no idea! My mother was great at making life an adventure so I just rolled with it. After an unsuccessful intervention, we came home to our 9th eviction notice and ended up moving in with my grandparents. I would just like to interject here and thank my grandparents and all our family/friends who stepped up to help us during that hard time.

In one day, I lost everything! My home, my dad and then also my mom because she went back to work 12 hours a day trying to support us. I can say the church definitely rallied around my mom as half the people at my dad's intervention were from church. They helped us move and supportive friends gave my mom money. We continued life as normal, only for me, NOTHING WAS NORMAL! I was suddenly very alone, I felt abandoned, lost and angry. My little 10-year-old heart was broken at the loss of my family; no more dance lessons and all of a sudden "we can't afford it" was a common phrase I heard. My grandparents did the best they could to love us but I found myself alone at home a lot while my mom was working. The friendships with my siblings were tight and we rallied together but I was so heartbroken. I was baptized at age 12 not really feeling the Lord in my heart. It was expected that I got baptized so I just went through the motions. I knew from all the lessons and church retreats I attended that God loved me but never really "felt" him. The power of the Holy Spirit wasn't even mentioned at church. I used to read books in church because I was bored (sorry Aunt Jane) and didn't really feel connected to Him. How could God's love enter a place filled with anger, frustration and hurt?

Foundations

I am sure there were people trying to help me but I just didn't want to hear it.

My high school days could have been worse. I got all A's and B's and was active in sports. My heart continued to be empty but I attended all the church activities and camps that were available to me. I made some really great friends who kept me out of trouble (thank you Christi, Doug and Robbie). It was expected of me to go to college, so with amazing scholarships from my church denomination, I attended Chapman University in Orange, California.

College was fun and I had heard of an amazing program to study abroad in France. So, my junior year of college, I packed up a suitcase and headed to Cannes, France. I was going there to break up the monotony of school and to have a little fun and adventure. Studying other people and cultures was fascinating to me, (I did marry a man from South Africa), and since I had been studying the French language for over 5 years, France seemed like a good fit. Little did I know that God was calling me back to Him during that time. First semester, I lived in Cannes, France in the third story of an international college overlooking a white sand beach with crystal-clear water. It was amazing!! My younger sister joined me on this first semester adventure and we studied the French language 9AM-12PM and then hit the beach for the afternoon. Travel, eat, beach, repeat! I loved it! My heart was filled with adventure but I still didn't know God.

I went home for the holidays to see friends and family and then headed to Paris (by myself- without my sister) for second semester. Because of my

Foundations

Christmas detour home, I joined a different study abroad program two weeks tardy. Friendships had already been established and I suddenly found myself in a foreign country again and this time completely alone! No one wanted to be my friend or took the time to meet me. Let me just tell you, I am fun and a very funny person (ha-ha) and it was devastating to me that no one wanted to even give me the time of day. I lived with a Parisian family who welcomed me because by that time I spoke fluent French, but my heart again was sad and lonely. I cried myself to sleep many nights. It was on a quiet night in Boulogne, France in February of 1997 that I finally cried out to God to help me. I was so sad and so lonely it was overwhelming!! It was there, for the first time, I heard the Lord answer me and felt Him enter my heart.

Everyone knows the popular bible verse Jeremiah 29:11, "For I know the plans I have for you, declares the LORD, plans for welfare, and not for evil, to give you a future and a hope." However, my favorite scripture is Jeremiah 29: 12-13, "Then you will call upon me and come and pray to me, and I will hear you. You will seek me and find me when you seek me with all your heart."

I just love that! I basically said to God, "God, I know you're there and I'm sad and alone. I'm in this amazing place and completely alone and heartbroken. Please help me! Go with me Lord." From that point on there was a shift in my attitude and I thought to myself, I don't need anyone but God. I felt HIM for the very first time enter into my heart and He was with me. I was taking a French architecture class where we met at a different monument 3 times a week to study its design. Just

Foundations

me and God trucking through Paris; learning and absorbing the culture. I was never alone and that empty feeling had left me. I had saved all my money for my two-week spring break and so God and I took a train ride to the high cliffs off the Italian coast and ate lobster and drank wine. We went to Switzerland together and took a boat ride in Germany. Just me and God and for the first time in my life, my heart was filled. Looking back, I think how crazy it was to travel throughout Europe for two weeks alone at the age of 21; but I wasn't alone and it was amazing! God was with me. I did attend some church services in French and that was amazing. God was making himself relational and it was amazing to know Him that way. Sadly, I never opened my Bible

I came back to the states a new person only no one really knew about my new found relationship with God. I wasn't a self-starter (at the time) and so it never dawned on me to open my bible or attend church to continue my relationship with God. I definitely wasn't encouraged by anyone to attend church or grow in a relationship with God during that time. Funny (insert sarcasm here), I thought it was someone else's responsibility to mentor me in a relationship with Christ. Nope! That would be ALL ME!!

I graduated with a degree in French and a minor in Sociology. Sadly, with no direction or focus in my life, I thought, what's next? I had friends encourage me to attend a massage therapy course which I did end up taking and LOVED! My older sister then nudged me to move to Georgia to be with her, so I packed up everything I owned and moved there to start my massage therapy career!

Foundations

It was within a month of living in Georgia that I met my Husband Sean. I started a massage business there and to supplement my income, I worked as a floor trainer at a local gym making $5.25/hour (how funny is that! Gas was also 69 cents per gallon back then, but I digress). I was minding my own business one evening, at the gym, when a large (muscular) man walked in. As he turned to walk away from me, I fell to the floor instantly! Not knowing who he was or what was happening, I thought to myself "this man is going to change my life." I have been married to Sean Coetzee, my smart, charming and big-hearted husband now for 21 years and I thank God each day He brought him into my life. I used to be a terrible listener so God had to knock me to my knees to know that Sean was the man He had for me. I do remember praying for a husband in church as a kid and really do feel that the Lord made Sean just for me (Thank you Lord).

We began our life together in the small town of Peachtree City, Georgia. We started attending church together because of his parent's influence and it wasn't long before I was back on the church track going every Sunday. After our first year of marriage, Sean started his own business. We began to have children and life was plugging away. We had the new house, 2 cars, 2 kids and a business and life was good! Sadly, I don't think we ever opened our Bibles (the what?). We even hosted bible study groups at our home but even those felt empty.

After 6 years of owning his own granite and custom cabinet business, Sean was ready to move on and it was here that we had our first call from the Lord. "Move to Hawaii!" What you would think was a

Foundations

great call was very scary to us and far from family. Sean's brother had married a girl from Hawaii and we had family ties to them but we were looking to move to Oahu and they were set up on the Big Island. With no support from my family, we decided to NOT move to Hawaii. BIG MISTAKE! We decided to stay in Georgia; purchasing 2 old junky houses to renovate and sell. If you're old enough to know, this was 2007, the year with a huge housing crash and we found ourselves deeply in debt; 3 houses, 2 kids and 2 cars and ZERO INCOME. Our credit cards were maxed out with no wiggle room to downsize. We thought we could sell the 2 houses but no one was buying. The housing market had crashed and with it, we were crashing too! With nothing left to do, a business opportunity from Sean's brother (thank you Christian and Jodi) opened up and like our call at the beginning of 2007, we ended up moving to Hawaii.

Do you remember I said in the beginning, when God calls you to do something, you might as well do it right away? He's got a great way of getting you where He needs you to be no matter what you think.

Man were things good in Hawaii! It's sunny, warm and of course there's the beautiful ocean and culture. Sean's business was flourishing and his parents soon moved to the Big Island with his brother. Me and the kids were traveling back and forth to the mainland for weddings and baby showers. We had yearly passes to the water park and of course the most beautiful beaches you have ever seen at our availability. Things were amazing but at the same time very stressful. Sean worked 13-15 hours a day; I felt like a single mom, money was always tight but it always came in. We were supporting a very expensive mistake back in Georgia still hanging on to the 3 houses and don't forget those fun credit cards that were maxed out.

We joined a local church, attended each Sunday and was a part of home groups but again, I don't think we ever opened our bibles. Poor God, He was just calling and calling us time and time again and we never made the effort. I'm sure you don't feel sorry for me as I was working barely 10 hours a week, both kids in school and living in Hawaii. Yes, it was amazing but at the same time we had to fight for every dollar we made. We would get a $20,000 check in and waiting next to the computer was $20,001 worth of bills. I was driving all over Oahu Friday afternoons at 4PM to get a check in the bank to make payroll by 5PM and my stress was through the roof. I was so bad at what we were doing!! I couldn't handle it. Where was my faith? Where was my trust? We left behind a HUGE financial disaster in Georgia but fortunately, by the grace of God, were able to pay for everything. We were just skimming by and stress between Sean and I was HIGH. I began to be resentful; he was gone all day working so hard for us and to also clear out the debt we had from Georgia. I felt alone. We went into more debt to grow his new granite business but that was just too heavy for me to bear! We were up to our eyeballs in debt and I just felt like I was drowning.

Did I mention I didn't handle the stress well? This is where biblical life skills would have been so valuable, yet, I had none. Sean was a master at it. He worked so hard and long hours and was flourishing. His stress was high but he knew it was part of being a business owner. Unfortunately, I was

Foundations

just getting more and more resentful at life. There had to be more to this life than just working your butt off to barely get by. I didn't want that and after years of nagging Sean at this new found stressful life, he didn't want it either. I cried out to the Lord one Sunday night in August of 2011, "Lord save us, we are drowning and we don't know how to stop this freight train of a business Sean's made and it owns us and controls our everything, SAVE US!" and I kid you not, from the back of my spirit I heard this still small voice say, "ok, but you are going to have to give up Hawaii." Ok Lord, "yes I will," I replied. Remember Jeremiah 29:13-15, I am always so touched how God keeps hearing my cries.

Thus, began the best/worst 5 months of our entire lives. We didn't know how but we wanted help to get out of the stress. God knew. Two days after my cry to God, Sean came home from work with chest pain and shortness of breath. He was 34 and having a heart attack! We rushed him to the ER and was told THANKFULLY he was NOT having a heart attack. They began to run tests on his heart, lungs, body functions, etc. All came back normal. EKG's, stress tests, spinal tap, sleep studies, ALL NORMAL! Fortunately, his amazing family (thank you Kona family) came over from the Big Island and helped run the business while Sean began to experience these very weird and life freezing symptoms. He would sleep 20 hours a day only getting up to eat and then return to bed. He was mute for an afternoon unable to speak. He had seizures that put him on the floor for minutes at a time and again and again, all medical test came back "normal." It was during this time that we began to hear from the Lord and for the first time EVER, WE OPENED OUR BIBLES!! God began to speak to us.

God, "I've got you."
Me, "but Lord, we owe so much money."
God, "don't worry, trust Me."
God, "I am doing a new thing."
God, "I'm going to release you from your strongholds."
God, "I am yours and you are Mine."
God, "Revelations 3: 1-2, I know your works. You have the reputation of being alive, but are dead (spiritually). Wake up, and strengthen what remains and is about to die, for I have not found your works complete in the sight of my God."

In my mind, God was calling us out on our lack of relationship with Him. I like the Easy English Standard version best; Revelations 3: 1-2, "I know everything that you do. I know that people praise you. They think that you are alive. But you are dead in your spirit. Wake up! Your lives as believer are nearly dead! You must become strong again."

The Lord was so right (of course), we were over the top blessed in our life in Hawaii and at the same time, knowing God called us there, we were terrible Christians. How could I be so stressed out if I trusted the Lord. "Be anxious about nothing and pray without ceasing" (Philippians 4: 6-7), I NEVER DID THIS!! These were things I heard of but never did. For the first time, Sean and I repented and again, handed our lives over to the Lord. We were making a disaster of things and didn't want to be in charge anymore. The Bible was alive and spoke truth into our lives for the first time.

God, "I am taking you to a new land, where I will guide your steps and renew you and Sean is to do nothing but read the Bible."

Foundations

God was calling us into relationship with HIM. 35 years old, attending church my ENTIRE LIFE and God was like "girl, wake up, I am here, you don't even know me!! You don't open your bible or pray for people. You attend church, worship with your hands held high and YOU DON'T EVEN KNOW WHO I AM!!" I was a lukewarm Christian and devastated with this realization.

All of these things we began to hear from the Lord. He spoke to us every day; in between the ER visits, seizures and long naps. He comforted us with His scriptures and His word. He told us things about where we were going and where we would live and began to give us dreams and vision of another place and time. He was wanting to set us free. A freedom only Christ can provide. To be in this world but not OF this world. We chased money, cars, and travel. We did things in our own power and not His. For the first time, it felt right! God was back with me/us, guiding and counseling us and moving us to a different place; a place with Him! Hawaii is an expensive place to live and so we decided to move to Bend, Oregon where we could take our family to rest and recover. Sean's unexplained symptoms dissipated the second we hit Oregon ground.

God miraculously cleansed us from expensive debts we owed on a building we were leasing in Hawaii, all debts from Georgia were gone, no medical bills remained and we moved to Oregon to heal. Only God can make that happen! Sean and I spent years on the couch of a counselor's office "cleaning out the rubble," we called it. Some very tough and ugly conversations were had but they had to happen in order to restore our marriage. We began to see, hear and feel the power of the Lord move in our lives. Love, grace and kindness replaced frustration, resentment and irritation. Scriptures had meaning to them and we were introduced to the Holy Spirit. Sean didn't work for over 2 years and all he did was drive the kids to and from school and read the Bible. This was exactly what God told us He would do! I truly believe it was God that saved us that August day back in 2011. We cried out to Him and He heard us and He saved us!

We've spent the last 9 years of our life being cleansed and restored into the people God wants us to be. Our priorities are in check and we are so grateful to God for His love. I've been released from strongholds and untruths that I believed about myself that God didn't want me to carry. He's healed my broken heart from the loss of my family as a child. He's told me I'm beautiful and given me a new heart to love people in the way He loves them. He took the broken, bitter, stressed out, unable-to-cope girl I used to be and restored her to a joy-filled, God honoring women full of love and kindness (trying my best anyways). He healed my husband too! He's been healed from disappointments he's carried all his life, brokenness in his heart from failures and unaccomplished dreams. God restored our marriage, setting us free from resentment, anger and bitterness. God's given us a new dream and I know it's beginning with this book. My husband will one day lead a church and I plan to sit front row in full support.

God wants us to share with you our story of restoration and reconciliation; or is it reconciliation and restoration? God wants to be reconciled with YOU! He's probably been calling after you for a long time but you haven't heard Him or if you were like

Foundations

me, you were a terrible listener. That's all He ever really wanted anyway; was to be known by you. Face it, without Him, we are just broken. You may think you've got it together and can fake it all you want. You need Him and He wants you! I was a lukewarm Christian. I knew about faith but had none. I knew God was my provider but freaked out when we needed money. I knew the Lord's prayer but never prayed. I was angry, sad and bitter instead of joy-filled, loving and kind. God truly changed my life! I needed to be saved; I needed a Savior!

Life is hard, families are tough, and relationships are complex. God has stuff to say about all of that! "He is the Way, the Truth and the Life" (John 14:6)! Before August of 2011, I was only aware of the Lord and now I know Him. He is kind and loving and wants to know you too! He's taught me so much about Him, life and myself that I feel you need some encouragement too in how to move forward towards spiritual maturity with HIM! I want to share what I've learned so that you too can know our Heavenly Father. Has He been calling you the way He was calling me? Are you listening or maybe you are just halfway doing this "God thing?" Let's change that! Let's take the time and make the effort to be reunited with our King. He's given us so much, it's time now for us to be strongly united back to Him for future generations to come.

For the next 30 days I pray and encourage you to lean into the Lord. Open your Bible. Pray. Knowing these foundational truths about God will not only grow you in spiritual maturity but it will grow you into a loving relationship with the Lord.
Let's get started!

Foundations

Day 1: The Fall

It's a Christian term used that describes the transition of the first man and woman (Adam and Eve) from a state of oneness and obedience with God to a separated state and disobedience. In the Garden of Eden, the man and woman could eat of all the fruit from all the trees except the Tree of Life. In this tree was the knowledge of good and evil. They were innocent with God until the serpent (Satan) tricked Eve into eating its fruit; which of course, like a good wife, she shared with Adam. God had created man in His image to be light and free from knowing of evil. Like a child who knows they've done something wrong, Adam and Eve hid from God and sin entered the story. Sadly, what was intended for a love story, Satan destroyed. God's desire was to be with you and love you. When evil entered between God and man, God immediately planned to save us through the blood of Jesus. God desires to be reunited with his first loves! You see the story of God is actually a redemptive love story. The good news is (spoiler alert) in the end, LOVE wins!

Scriptures:

Genesis 3, Romans 5: 12, 1 Corinthians 15: 21-22
Reflective questions:

1. What was God's reaction to Adam and Eve eating from the tree? What do you think about his reaction?
2. How could our lives have been different without sin?
3. Name a time you have been tricked/deceived. What were the consequences? How did you feel?

Foundations

Foundations

Day 2   Repentance

Ugg, this is such an intimidating word for those who don't hear it very often. I hate to start with this but to move forward in Christ, you must first repent. The google dictionary says that to repent is to feel or express sincere regret or remorse about one's wrongdoing or sin. In a noncomplicated way, it just means to acknowledge you did wrong and say you're sorry. The first thing we must do to accept Jesus into our heart is to repent. We must admit (out loud) that we are sinners and have faults and that we need a Savior. Sick people need a doctor; broken people need a Savior.   There must also be remorse in our repentance; a true understanding of wrong deepens the desire to unite with our Lord. Without admitting we are sinners; we are arrogant and repentance is empty. We are all sinners and if you think you aren't, ask your closest friend. Ha! I don't know why people have such a hard time admitting they are wrong. It's not a big secret. We all mess up or make mistakes. So just admit it, you are not perfect and that's ok.

When sin entered the world, it began our devastating separation from God. The good news is that He wants you back! So, say you're sorry for the things you have done and receive His forgiveness!

Scriptures:
Job 42:6, Matthew 3: 2, 5-6, Matthew 4:17, Mark 2:17, Luke 13:3

Reflective questions:
1. What does repentance mean to you?
2. Check your heart, are you truly remorseful?
3. Think of a time you said you were sorry to someone. How did that affect your relationship? Now relate it to your relationship

Foundations

with the Lord. How has it changed your relationship with Him?

_____
_____
_____
_____
_____
_____
_____
_____
_____
_____
_____
_____
_____
_____
_____
_____
_____
_____
_____
_____
_____
_____
_____
_____
_____
_____
_____
_____
_____
_____

Foundations

Day 3 Forgiveness

Forgiveness is being released from one's trespasses or wrongdoings. Once we repent (say we're sorry), we can let go of our sin and know that we are forgiven. Free from the transgressions, guilt and shame we may carry from our wrongdoings. God sent his son, Jesus, down to earth in human form to die on a cross and 3 days later rise in order to pay the price of our sins. It is through the blood of Jesus that we are forgiven. Receive His forgiveness. This is crucial to your growth in Christ.

In the Lord's prayer, Jesus gives his disciples an example on how to pray and one of the very important things He says is forgive us our sins as we forgive those who sin against us. It's a two-part instruction. It's asking the Lord to forgive us as well as we need to forgive others. It's just as important for us to forgive others in the same manner in which we were forgiven. When we receive Christ in our hearts and repent, we immediately receive forgiveness. You are forgiven and you should forgive others. Selah! (meditate on that).

Scriptures:

Psalm 32:1, Matthew 6: 12, 14-15, Colossians 2:13, Colossians 3:13, 1 John 1:9

Reflective questions:

1. How has knowing you are forgiven changed your relationship with God?
2. Are you holding back forgiveness from someone who needs it or has asked for it?
3. Think of an example where you had to forgive someone. How did it positively affect you? Negatively affect you?

Foundations

Foundations

Day 4 Baptism

You've repented, you've been forgiven, now it's time to be baptized. Being baptized in water is important to your Christian walk. It's declaring publicly that you are now a believer in Christ. Being submerged in water represents the cleansing of one's sins. Re-emerging out of the water represents the new creation you've become in Christ. The entire submersion is a representation of Christ dying for the forgiveness of your sins on the cross and 3 days later being raised from the dead. Christ defeated death and so have you! You will now spend eternity with Jesus in heaven. Baptism is an outward act of faith saying you are dying to one's self and being renewed in who Jesus is making you to be. Even Jesus was baptized publicly before He began his earthly ministry. He was publicly declaring his life to be for the Father. If you haven't made that step yet, please reach out to a local Christian church and set up a time to declare you are the Lord's.

Scriptures:
Isaiah 42:9, Matthew 3: 5-6 and 13-17, 2 Corinthians 5: 17

Reflective questions:
1. What happened to Jesus once He was baptized?
2. When did you get baptized and how did it change you?
3. Are you truly God's? What in your "old life" are you hanging onto that God wants you to get rid of?

Foundations

Foundations

Day 5   Mercy

This idea of receiving mercy is very foreign to people because it's so hard to truly accept that you get it for FREE! Mercy is receiving all the lovingkindness, forgiveness and redemptive power of the Lord even when we don't deserve it. It's hard to receive when you come from a world without love. Mercy and steadfast love are very interchangeable in scripture. God loves you so much that He sent His only son to die for you. YOU! Prior to Jesus, you had the law of Moses and it required sacrifice and very few people had access to God. Through Jesus Christ, we thankfully, automatically get access to Him. Jesus paid the price for us. He's calling you back to Him and He does that with mercy and love. Although we receive it, there's nothing we can do to earn it. It's just there, a gift for us from God allowing us to fully receive everything and ALL that He is!   God is everything. He is the GREAT I AM! He is kind, full of compassion and wants to show you His desire to be with you. He's calling you back and there's nothing you can do that would cause Him to withhold anything from you. NOTHING! Once God is in your heart, He's there forever.   Receive the mercy He's offering and allow it to flow in your heart to others.

Scriptures:
Exodus 3:13-14, 1 Chronicles 16:34, Psalm 130: 7, Proverbs 3:3, Matthew 9:13, Ephesians 2:4-5, Hebrews 4:16

Reflective questions:
1. What is lovingkindness? What is steadfast love?
2. How has receiving mercy from God molded you? Do you act differently?

Foundations

3. Do you find it's easy or hard to give mercy/kindness to others? Ask God to show you how you can do it better.

Foundations

Day 6   Grace

Grace, the most beautiful gift given to us by God. It's his abundant love, favor and blessings poured out over us. Grace, like mercy, is undeserved; we can do nothing to receive it. God loves us so much that He's willing to bless us each and every day. The way the Lord loves you is by giving you grace. Grace is like a VIP ticket to God. It's an all-access pass to the savior, the creator of the heavens and earth. In the bible, depending upon your translation, the word grace can be substituted with favor. To have God's favor means that you are his priority and He's chasing after you to give you His very best. It also means that you can live a life free of stress knowing you are His favorite! He's with you and you with Him. Receiving grace will ensure you always have what you need at the moment you need it and that it will be enough.

Scriptures:
Psalm 45:2, Psalms 84:11, Romans 5:17, 2 Corinthians 13:14, Ephesians 2:8-9
Reflective questions:
1. What does God's grace mean to you?
2. What is the difference between grace and mercy?
3. How do you pay it forward to others?

Foundations

Foundations

Day 7 Faith

Another tricky concept of Christianity is faith. It's complete trust and confidence in a person and for Christians this is a person we can't even see. Though He walked the earth as a man for many decades, He died and went to be seated at the right hand of God in heaven. It's a tough concept to wrap your mind around and then live by. We are to live by faith. You are to grow yourself in faith toward the Lord in complete confidence while trusting He is who He says He is. Giving your life over to Christ means you have faith in who He is and the power He possesses. He is there! He sees you! He knows the hairs on your head are numbered. Did you know that having faith is a spiritual gift? Having faith is something you receive only once you have allowed God to enter your heart. It allows your eyes to be opened to the truth in the scriptures and believe! Each one of us receives faith when we believe, so ask God to grow your faith in Him and see how wonderful He can be.

Scriptures:
Luke 12:7, Luke 17:5-6, Romans 1:16-17, Romans 10:17, 2 Corinthians 5:7, Hebrews 11:1
Reflective questions:
1. What does "the righteous shall live by faith" mean to you?
2. What can you do today to allow God to grow your faith?
3. Think of a time when someone shared their faith with you? How did it affect you?

_____
_____

Foundations

Foundations

Day 8 Holy Spirit

Before Jesus ascended into heaven to sit at the right hand of God, He promised the disciples He would send them the Holy Spirit. They were told to go to Jerusalem and wait for this gift. They were to be baptized with the Holy Spirit. The Holy Spirit is part of the trinity; the God head three in one. Being baptized in the Holy Spirit opens another connection for us to the Father. It enables us to do what Jesus did; heal the sick, give sight to the blind and cast out demons. The Holy Spirit is our helper, our counselor. When we receive Him, He comes IN us and UPON us and we receive His power. It's how we complete the mission of Christ in the world. He draws us closer to Christ by convicting us of sin and encouraging us to be more like Him. He helps our eyes to be opened to the wisdom of the scriptures and causes it to come to life. If we seek the Holy Spirit's guidance, we will better see God's will for our lives. It is the fulfilled promise in the scripture of the power given to us by God for the glorifying and edification of the kingdom. If you have yet to be baptized in the Holy Spirit, say this prayer with me: "Father God, baptize me with the Holy Spirit. He is in me and upon me. Give me supernatural wisdom and knowledge from the Holy Spirit and let my heart be filled with power. I want to do the wonders and miracles that Jesus did and I receive Him. Amen."

Scripture:

Luke 24:49, John 1:33-34, Acts 1:4-5 & 8, Acts 2:4, Acts 4:31, 1 Corinthians 2:10-13
Reflective questions:
1. When were you baptized with the Holy Spirit? How did it change your walk with Christ?

Foundations

2. Is there a friend you know who believes in God but not the power of the Holy Spirit? Ask God to give you words to encourage them to be baptized in the Holy Spirit.
3. What power has the Holy Spirit given you for the glory of the kingdom?

Foundations

Day 9 Spiritual Gifts

Now that the Holy Spirit has come upon you, Jesus says He will give you power and certain gifts for the edification of the kingdom of God. The gifts of the spirit are as follows: faith, preaching/teaching, prayer, speaking in tongues, interpreting those words, wisdom, knowledge, gifts of healings, miracles, prophesying and discerning of spirits. Spiritual gifts are a part of God's grace. He will equip us with what we need at the right time when we need it. The Holy Spirit will distribute these gifts in order to fulfill the ministry at hand. These gifts, like grace, are not earned and should not promote spiritual pride when used. We should have a willing heart to accept each gift according to its need for the love and encouragement to others. If you need faith, ask to be filled with faith. If you're gifted with prayer, use it to lift up and encourage others in their journey. Our gifts should be shared with others and be used for the betterment of the church. I feel you have a sense of responsibility with your spiritual gifts to bestow them on others so they too, will share in the joy of the good news!

Scriptures:
1 Corinthians 12:4-11, Romans 12:4-8, 1 Peter 4:10-11, 1 Timothy 4:14
Reflective questions:
1. What are your spiritual gifts? (If you don't know, go online and take a free spiritual gifts assessment- just google free spiritual test).
2. How and when do you use your spiritual gifts?
3. For whom are the spiritual gifts?

Foundations

Foundations

Day 10 Fruit of the Spirit

The fruit of the spirit is love, joy, peace, patience, kindness, goodness, faithfulness, gentleness and self-control. Does that describe you? It definitely did NOT describe me until I was baptized in the Holy Spirit. You see, God wants us to live a life filled with joy and kindness towards others. He wants us to get rid of rudeness, lies and deceit and be gentle, good and faithful. To live in the flesh is to live jealous, angry and full of hate but to live in the spirit is to transition to a life overflowing with abundant love, joy and self-control. As you're growing in the fruit of the spirit, you will see the Holy Spirit begin to slowly reshape and remold you (and I'm sorry but yes, it's sometimes very painful). God wants you to be renewed in your mind, heart and soul. As He "removes the rubble", as I like to call it, you will see a positive shift in your life. He's cleansing you of the "old you" and making you a new person in Him. The Holy Spirit will guide you towards union with Him.   God does not want us to be "unclean" or negative, He gives us the fruit of the spirit to guide us into His likeness. He directs us every step of the way towards a life of freedom, love and peaceful living. We must recognize that without the gift of the Holy Spirit, it's impossible to be filled with the fruit of the spirit and live as Christ intends. We must acknowledge we need Him to help us become who He intended us to be.

Scriptures:

Romans 15:13, Galatians 5:22-24, Ephesians 4:2
Reflective questions:
1. What fruit of the spirit is easy for you to exude?
2. Which one (or two) do you need work on?

Foundations

3. How can you live better according to the fruit of the spirit?

Foundations

Day 11 God is Love

It's so important to really grasp this concept of God's infinite love for us. God so loved the world that He gave His only begotten son. He LOVED US from the beginning. He made the choice to love us unconditionally. He sent His son to die on a cross for us so we wouldn't be overcome by our sins. He saved YOU! He LOVES YOU! More than you could ever know, He wants to spend eternity with you in heaven. God's greatest commandment is to love HIM. Then He tells us to love others as we love ourselves. This idea of loving others, especially strangers, can sometimes take time and it may not come naturally. The devil is really good at his job of deception; and can create a lot of havoc in our relationships with others. As the Holy Spirit removes anger, frustration and other negativity from your heart, it creates a space for God's unlimited love to take root. You love God, love others and love yourself. Yes! God even calls you to love yourself. Not in a narcissistic way but by having a content expression of self-love. It's also realizing who you are and confidently loving yourself because Christ lives in you. As you grow and mature in your Christlikeness, you will see others as God sees them and you will love them too.

Scriptures:
John 3:16, John 15:12-17, 1 Corinthians 13:4-13, 1 John 4:7-10 & 16 & 19
Reflective questions:
1. What is love? From where does is come?
2. What do you think about God's call to love others?
3. Do you love yourself? Describe what that means to you?

Foundations

Foundations

Day 12 Trinity

Understanding the Trinity is key to understanding who God is. The word comes from "tri" which means three and "unity" meaning one. God was in the world and the spirit of God was with Him. God in the flesh became Jesus, so He could model a life completely free of sin. He was tempted in every way and yet was sinless. He is perfect! Jesus, then died on a cross and defeated death; by raising from the dead 3 days later. His position is next to God. So, God took Jesus back up to heaven to be with Him and sent us the Holy Spirit. The Holy Spirit is with us and upon us. The Holy Spirit is Jesus and God in one. They are different beings but the same in God. God is three distinct individuals; God the Father in heaven, Jesus, the son of God and the Holy Spirit, God's power upon us. God didn't want us to live separate from him. He wants all people to have access to him. Praise God for Jesus and the Holy Spirit who connect all three into one.

Scriptures:

Matthew 28:19, John 10:30, John 14: 9-11, 1 Corinthians 8:6, 2 Corinthians 13:14, Colossians 2:9

Reflective questions:

1. Do you fully comprehend the God head three in one? Write down any confusion and ask God to show you the truth about it.
2. How do you explain the Trinity to non-believers?
3. Who is God, Jesus Christ and the Holy Spirit to you? Do they have different roles in your life?

Foundations

Foundations

Day 13 Pray

To pray is to talk with God. This is a foundational step towards closeness with Him. It's reciprocal communication between you and the Father. You speak to Him and He speaks to you. Take time to be quiet and listen; for our Father speaks to our hearts. God says we should pray without ceasing. He wants us to make our requests known to Him. Talk with God when you're in the car, walking the aisles at the store, sitting in your chair at work. Communication is key to any and all relationships. If you need help praying, Jesus gave us an example on how to do it in the Lord's prayer. The Lord's prayer includes thanksgiving, supplication for others and His will to be made known to us. It includes forgiveness to ourselves and to others and request for protection from the devil. It's a model prayer but you have the freedom to come to God, as you are, and speak directly with Him for your needs, wants and desires. God is a loving Father and even though He knows of the things you need before you need them; He still wants you to come to Him with those requests. Go to the Father and spend quiet time with Him in prayer. He wants you to pray for yourself, your neighbors, your country, it's leaders and yes, even your enemies. Also, consider asking God how you can serve him today instead of asking him for a personal need. Wait and see what will happens!

Scriptures:

Matthew 5:44, Matthew 6:6-13, 1 Thessalonians 5:17, James 5:16

Reflective questions:

Foundations

1. How much time do you spend praying? How can you improve?
2. Who and what consumes your prayers?
3. What are some results of prayer?

Foundations

Day 14 Ask and Receive

As your communication increases with our loving God, you will begin to see who He truly is. He is loving, full of compassion and a heavenly Father who wants to bless you! Ask and you will receive. God wants to give you the desires of your heart. He is our Father, our Dad. What father wouldn't want to bless and give gifts to his children? You must ask for it and then wait. If you request falls in line with the perfect will of God, then you will receive it. Selfish wants and needs that feed the flesh, tend to not fall in line with the Lord's purpose. With union between God's will and your desires; you can be confident you will receive that which you ask. Expectantly anticipate all you need from the Father in heaven whose ways are above our ways and who promises to provide for us. He defeated death! He can heal the sick, of course He can bless you with the desires of your heart. As you grow into Christ-likeness, your desires will coincide with God's desires for your life. There is a commitment on our side to trust and believe that what we ask for we will receive. There is a confidence in our heavenly Father that guarantees our request will be heard and fulfilled. Hope and patiently wait on God to show up! You may not receive something you've asked for immediately (sometimes you do) but commit your ways to the Lord and know you will receive it!

Scriptures:

Psalm 37:3-5, Matthew 7:7-11, Matthew 21:22, Philippians 4:19

Reflective questions:
1. What prayer are you patiently waiting for God to answer?
2. What are you learning while you wait?

Foundations

3. What blessings has God brought you that you knew were from Him?

Foundations

Day 15 Community

In the book of Acts, we learn how God created us to be in community (church) with Him and with others. He had a very specific design for the church so each person would bring their God given skills and talents for the growth of the kingdom. One would preach, one would teach, one would lead, pray, etc. It takes many moving parts for a church to function and we all should be encouraged to serve. For when we serve each other in love and faith, we are also serving our heavenly Father. We should also support each other because life is not easy! Everyone faces tough trials and challenges and God created us to face those together. God does not want you to be alone. He may call you into a time of solitude but that's different than not having like-minded Christian friends in your life. We are to love, pray and encourage each other together in our Christian walk. You can learn a lot by watching and listening to a mature believer. If you are not a part of a local church or you don't have other Christian's in your life; ask God to bring you into community and He will show you where to go.

Scriptures:
Matthew 25:40, Acts: 2:44-47, 1 Corinthians 12:12-31, Galatians 6: 2
Reflective questions:
1. How are you active in community?
2. Is anything holding you back from going deeper into relationship with other Christians?
3. Is God asking you to feed into another believer? If not, ask God to show you someone who needs your friendship.

Foundations

Foundations

Day 16 Fellowship

Fellowship is a unity brought about by the Holy Spirit bonding the believers to the Lord and to each other. There is power in unity! Jesus says wherever two or more are gathered in His name, He is there! Things get serious and the spirit can really move and do good works when we are together in our beliefs and purpose. God uses the example of the body to show how we need to be together in our purpose. We are many members but one body. Each member has a specific function and purpose and it just doesn't work one without the other. We are to be the hands and feet of Jesus; unified together for the greatness and growth of the kingdom. We cannot move forward with a purpose without all the different moving parts pieced TOGETHER to work TOGETHER! The kingdom needs you; there is a role only you can fulfill.

Scriptures:
Matthew 18:19-20, Acts 2: 42-44, 1 Corinthians 1:10, 1 Corinthians 12: 14-20
Reflective questions:
1. What is God's promise when two or more gather in His name?
2. What do you think happens when there is not unity in a church's purpose?
3. How can you assist the church in creating better fellowship?

_____
_____
_____
_____
_____
_____

Foundations

Foundations

Day 17 Put God First

God is a jealous God. He says in the 10 commandments that there should be no other God but Him. It's the first and most important commandment and God mentions it first so that we will know there should be no idols, figures or treasures above Him. God does not want to compete with your job, your finances or your favorite past time hobby. Your priority should ALWAYS be to put God first! When we talk about this, we also need to recognize that an "idol" can be anything we want or crave more than we want our heavenly Father. It says in the Bible that where your treasure is, there will be your heart also. Is God your most valuable treasure? Are you thinking about Him all the time, wanting to honor Him, know Him, love Him? By putting God first, everything else in your life will fall into his perfect alignment. Take the time to be with Him first thing in the morning and see what a great day you will have being filled with His love, wisdom and knowledge.

Scriptures:
Exodus 20:2-6, Proverbs 1:7, Proverbs 8: 10-11, Matthew 6:21 & 33

Reflective questions:
1. How can you begin to put God first above and before everything else in your life?
2. What are your most valuable treasures?
3. Is an idol in your life? Pray and ask the Holy Spirit to reveal to you if there is.

_____
_____
_____

Foundations

Foundations

Day 18 Put off the Old

I just love the way God loves us. He wants such good things for us. He wants us to prosper and live a life that honors Him. It takes a lot of mental and spiritual work to do this but you're not alone; the Holy Spirit will help you! Prayerfully, each day, we are being called to not be who we used to be but who Christ is calling us to be. We've been saved by the blood of Jesus, so live like it!! Be kind, compassionate, full of love towards others. Ask the Holy Spirit to guide the work required to strip yourself of the negative things you carry and be renewed in your mind and spirit. Take time, read scripture and focus on molding your mindset to the positive things of Jesus. Rid yourself of evil thoughts, sensuality, envy and pride. Become like Christ who is pure, love and just!

Scriptures:
Jeremiah 29:11, Isaiah 43:18-19, Mark 7:21-22, Ephesians 4:22-24, Philippians 4:8-9

Reflective questions:
1. What part of your past are you still holding onto that God wants gone? Give it to him in prayer.
2. How has the Holy Spirit changed you? Has anyone noticed?
3. Do you focus on what is pure, lovely and commendable?

_____
_____
_____
_____
_____

Foundations

Foundations

Day 19 Seek Wisdom and Knowledge

We all want to be smart! No one wakes up each day saying "today, I think I will be a fool." The Bible has a lot to say about seeking wisdom and knowledge of the Lord. There are great mysteries into the kingdom of God and sadly not everyone will have their eyes opened to them. We must first ask for wisdom and knowledge and then know and trust that the Holy Spirit will give it to us along with understanding. It's not just knowing the answers to life's issues, but it's information into how the Lord works and what He wants for your life. It's beautiful information and should be counted as the most valuable thing God can give you. It will also preserve you, save you from many follies and keep you safe from harm. Seeking the wisdom and knowledge of the Lord will keep your path straight, and release you from tons of worldly drama. It's far more valuable than gold or silver.

Scriptures:
Psalm 37:23, Proverbs 3: 13-23 & 35, Proverbs 4
Reflective questions:
1. What does your heart seek?
2. What priceless information have you learned about the Lord?
3. Think of a time God's wisdom has saved/helped you out in a situation?

_____
_____
_____
_____
_____
_____
_____

Foundations

Foundations

Day 20 Satan's Plan

Who is Satan? He is known as the fallen angel; born from God but not in His likeness. He comes to distract you, sway you and trick you away from your Father and His plans for you. Steal, kill, destroy; these are the motives of the devil. He comes to steal your joy, kill all you're doing for the kingdom and destroy your life. He wants you in Hell with him. I grew up in a church where the only thing spoken of was God's love for us. There was no education into the opposition you face as a Christ follower. Satan wants to hinder you from the good works of the Father and keep your relationship from growing. He appears as the "adversary" to disrupt God's kingdom by causing trouble. Be dressed and ready for battle because the devil is trying to lie and deceive you every second he can. He can whisper little lies into your mind but knowing the truth will give you the strongest weapon to fight off those lies. Ever wonder where that voice inside your head that tells you you're worthless or you can't do it comes from? It's the lies of the devil. When you know God and His truths (by being in the word), you are equipped to combat those lies. With God nothing is impossible so why would you think you can't do it? Know who God is so that you have wisdom against the devil who tries to deceive you. The good news is God has already won the battle. He's victorious, so stand confident that Satan's deceptions in your life are lies and that God has the truth for you.

Scriptures:
Luke 1:37, John 10:10, Romans 8:31, James 4:7, 1 Peter 5:8,

Reflective questions:
1. How is Satan the opposite of God?

Foundations

2. How do you think God feels about Satan?
3. What are ways you can get the Devil to flee from you?

Foundations

Day 21 Spiritual Warfare

There is a war going on and it's not against flesh and blood. It's not against people, their views on life or different religions. For Christians, it's against the principalities of darkness and evil and it's known as Spiritual Warfare. We struggle with good versus evil, flesh versus spirit, right and wrong. It's happening all the time in your mind, your heart and the world around you. God says that we should seek wisdom, knowledge and turn from evil. He also says we should clothe ourselves in truth, righteousness, peace and faith. Being covered in God's word is the biggest way we protect ourselves from the enemy. Who is the enemy? It's the forces of hell, a powerful, yet invisible realm. We must take a ready stance, dressed for battle against this unseen, satanic structure. If you stand against it and turn from evil, the Lord says it will be healing to your flesh. God also says if you turn from evil, his eyes and ears will be upon you. He will see you and hear you! To fight the spiritual battle guarantees you a closeness with the Lord. You won't be afraid because God is with you. So, stand strong on the foundations of God and you will be victorious in your fight.

Scriptures:
Psalm 34:14-15, Psalm 97:10, Proverbs 3:7-8, Ephesians 6: 10-18

Reflective questions:

1. What are your biggest mental struggles? Find 3 scriptures that tell you the truth in those situations and memorize them!
2. How are you protecting yourself from the lies of the enemy? Do you understand God has already defeated the enemy?

Foundations

3. What are you doing to grow in Christ and turn from evil?

Foundations

Day 22 Untruths

The devil is feeding you lies day in and day out about who you are, what you are doing and where you are in your life. God will say one thing so of course the devil will say the opposite. You must learn to distinguish between what God says (truth)and what the devil tells you (lies). These are things I call "untruths." They are lies you believe about yourself that simply aren't true. How can I feel ugly when God says I am beautifully and wonderfully made? How can I feel worthless when God will leave the 99 to go find me when I'm lost? There is a constant feed from the world that says we need to be prettier, wear a certain thing and get the newest nicest next best thing. God says your clothes will not be in ruin and the things He provides for you are enough. Know God so you know the truth. Know what the bible says about you so when someone tells you differently or puts you down; you don't accept that into your heart and mind as truth. The way I distinguish between lies and truth is lies will bring frustration and irritation and the truth will bring peace and joy. You can also combat these lies by being in the word daily. You will learn to see what is of God and what is a lie. Knowing the scriptures is so important for this very reason; it brings truth to every circumstance so you know the truth and the truth will set you free. Free from the lies of this world and the devil. You will be free from the negative things people say about you and you won't accept it. There is freedom in these truths!

Scriptures:
Psalm 139:14, Matthew 6:25-30, Luke 15:4-6, John 8:31-32 & 44, 1 John 3:8
Reflective questions:

Foundations

1. What untruths do you believe about yourself?
2. What would God say about them? Write this down and keep it close.
3. What is something you can do today to start believing what God says about you and move away from the lies of this world?

Foundations

Day 23 Open your Bible

As a Christian, we actually have a lot of work to do spiritually. We have to fight the battle against evil, die to one's self, grow in faith, love and kindness, seek wisdom and knowledge. It can be very overwhelming! Don't panic, you have the Holy Spirit and of course, the word of God to help you. I think the biggest thing we can do to grow as Christians and accomplish the above is OPEN OUR BIBLES!! BE IN THE WORD! All scripture is of God, by God and for God. It all points to truth! It is active and alive! If you want to know how to fight evil; open your Bible! If you want to know how to better raise your kids; open your Bible! If you need help with your finances; open your Bible. God created everything so of course He is going to have the answers to everything! (Here are those exclamations I tend to over-use). Everything you need for successful living is in there. It takes discipline, focus and the Holy Spirit to open your Bible and read every day. Ask and receive, remember? Ask the Holy Spirit to fill you with the desire to grow in the word and watch how the scriptures come alive in your life.

Scriptures:

Deuteronomy 11:18-21, Psalm 119:11-16, Proverbs 3:1-2, 2 Timothy 3:16-17, Hebrews 4:12

Reflective questions:

1. What is hindering you from opening your bible and how can you get rid of it?
2. What is your "Bible time" routine? If you don't have one, create one and write it down. (Written goals tend to come to fruition more than unwritten ones do. Set reminders on your phone.)

Foundations

3. What does the Bible say we should do with God's word?

Foundations

Day 24 Rejoice

Rejoice in the Lord always! Not sometimes or sporadically but always! Celebrate God for the awesomeness that He is, the things He does and how He loves you. Show great joy to Him who set you free from sin and darkness. He is worthy of our praise and wants us to worship and celebrate Him. Are you grateful to the Lord? Do you show Him great joy or delight? A lot of scriptures pair rejoicing with singing. I, personally am a terrible singer but I don't think God cares. When we sing, I think He hears angels singing? I believe He sees me celebrating Him and is pleased (even if it hurts his ears). Did you know that God also rejoices over you!!?? He does!! He sings a song of gladness for you. His love for you is pouring out like a song He sings loudly. How great is that!? We worship a King who loves us and celebrates the fact that we are His?

Scriptures:
Psalm 33:1-3, Psalm 118:24, Psalm 145:1-3, Zephaniah 3:17

Reflective questions:
1. How do you rejoice in the Lord? What comes naturally? Singing? Dancing?
2. How does it make you feel to know God rejoices over you?
3. What are three things you can start doing to celebrate God?

_____
_____
_____
_____
_____

Foundations

Foundations

Day 25 Fear Not

Fear is real and is an enemy tactic to pull you away from God's very best. It's definitely not a fruit of the spirit. We sometimes get scarred and if you're anything like me, you freeze. When I don't know what to do, I do nothing. However, God does not want us to live in fear. He says time and time again to not be fearful and then He makes the promise that He will be with you. We serve a God who calls you to a life without fear. Why would we be scarred knowing our heavenly Father is always with us? No matter what you're going through, knowing you have God with you should give you the confidence to keep pressing forward. If God is for you then who can ever hurt you? No one! He won't let you get burned and He will never give you more than you can handle. He's given us the Holy Spirit as our helper. Ask and receive what you need from your Father in heaven and go for it! Let not an ounce of fear stand in the way of receiving the very best that God has for you.

Scriptures:
Joshua 1:9, Psalm 56:3-4, Psalm 118:6-7, Isaiah 41:10, Isaiah 43:1-5, Hebrews 13:6

Reflective questions:
1. Do you have fear in your life holding you back?
2. What does God say you should do when afraid?
3. What scriptures do you go in moments of uncertainty? Write them down.

_____
_____
_____
_____
_____

Foundations

Foundations

Day 26 Anxiety

In a society stricken with anxiety, God has a lot to say about it. To have anxiety is to be stricken with worry and or fear. It can be debilitating and ruin our day-to-day activities. There is a healthy anxiety or nervousness that comes with a job interview or public speaking. The rapid heartbeat never leave your home type of anxiety (and sometimes too much coffee) is not healthy. God doesn't want it to be a part of your life. Remember, we just learned that we should not have fear because God is always with us, right? If God created you and knows the end from the beginning then, we should be comforted knowing He's in control. If God is in control, then why worry, right? For a lot of us, it's not that easy. This is a hard concept to uphold because we live in a world where we must have total and complete control; in every situation! God will sometimes put us in tough situations where we don't know what to do and we have no choice but to wait on Him to show up. He is in charge! When that uncertainty arrives, pray, trust and look to the Lord for what you need. Take a deep breath and know that God has you in the palm of His hand. He's not going to let you fall. It's a conscious decision to put God in the driver's seat and let Him be in total control.

Disclosure: I do recognize there are serious issues with anxiety and those who have it must be under the care of a Doctor. I encourage those also to be a part of a serious pray group and be in the word daily!

Scriptures:

Proverbs 12:25, Isaiah 46:10, Philippians 4: 6-7, 2 Timothy 1:7

Foundations

Reflective questions:
1. Do you worry? About what? Do you trust God to be with you in your worry?
2. Do you think anxiety and control are related? How? Why?
3. Do you know someone struggling with anxiety? Pray for them.

Day 27 Give Thanks

We shouldn't be afraid or anxious and God says we should do all things with thanksgiving. Be grateful! It's all grouped together; rejoicing, trusting, prayer, repentance, forgiveness; you need one to have the others. Nothing pleases a parent more than when they hand their child a gift and they say "Thank you." To be thankful for God and what He's done for you is the ultimate gift to Him. When you're sad or scarred, try rattling off all the things you're grateful for and see how that immediately turns your thoughts around. It's hard to be grumpy when your voice speaks words of thanksgiving. I recommend always speaking these OUTLOUD! I have found that by declaring out loud things of thanksgiving, it staves off the enemy! Being thankful is also a part of rejoicing. It's acknowledging that all things are from God and for God and we're grateful for them. It's an emotion in our heart that allows us to go out and share with others the glory we've received in Christ. When we enter into our day with praise and thanksgiving, it creates a space for God's glory to shine in us for others to see.

Scriptures:
1 Chronicles 16:34, Psalm 100:4-5, Colossians 3:17, 1 Thessalonians 5:16-18, 1 Timothy 4:4-5

Reflective questions:
1. How do you express your thankfulness to God?
2. What are you thankful for? Make a list and keep in close.
3. What is the key to giving thanks even during the hard times?

Foundations

Foundations

Day 28 Light and Salt

We are all called to be the light for the kingdom of God. It's our job to love God and then go out into the world and love others. When the spirit of God is in you and your life begins to shift away from what the world deems acceptable; you're going to look a lot more like Jesus (light). Your friends will see that something is different about you. In the world, there is darkness and evil but the light outshines darkness in any room. When your spirit is filled with love, joy and kindness; people will see that and be drawn to it. Be ready to give them a reason to why you have hope and joy. We are also called to be the salt of the earth. Not like the modern phrase "to be salty" is to be cranky or upset. To be the salt means to purposefully act in a such a way that others will see the unconditional love of Christ in you. You will model Christ likeness. Salt is a preservative and it's used to enhance flavor. Metaphorically speaking, we are purified with salt (the word of God) and then sent to be examples of God. We are loyal, flavorful believers shining bright for others to see.

Scriptures:
Matthew 5:13-16, 1 Peter 3:13-17

Reflective questions:
1. How do you model "salt" in your life?
2. Do you think your insides match your outsides?
3. During the day, how often do you consider whether or not people see you as a Christ follower? How are you behaving?

_____
_____
_____
_____

Foundations

Foundations

Day 29 Trust

Do you fully trust God with your life? Do you give him control over every aspect of it; like your spouse, your kids, your job and your finances? Or do you invite God to rule over simple things like where to vacation or what clothes you are going to wear to that big meeting? The biggest way we put our trust in God is by letting him be our leader IN ALL ASPECTS OF OUR LIVES! What you think you're in control of, you're actually not! Sorry to be the bearer of this bad news but the good news is that God is! He knows the ending from the beginning. For a lot of us control freaks, it's hard to take up our mat every single day and just allow God to be in charge. When we try and make sense of things, it could lead to a lot of frustration. God says to not rely on what we know. When was the last time you handed the events of your day over to God's leading? I wonder why that's so hard for us to do? I would much rather allow God to lead my life than me. I am with faults and mess things up big time yet it's still hard to give Him my total trust. There's great freedom in allowing God to lead your life. Freedom from worry, stress and uncertainty. You carry none of those things when you trust that your heavenly Father's in control. Trust Him and see where He will take you.

Scriptures:
Psalm 37:3, Proverbs 3:5-6, Isaiah 12:2, Isaiah 46:10, Isaiah 50:10

Reflective questions:
1. How do you show your trust in God?
2. Where in your life, do you need to hand control over to God?

Foundations

3. What role does the Holy Spirit play in increasing/decreasing your trust?

Foundations

Day 30 The Great Commission

To love God and love others is one of our most valuable jobs as Christians. We are called or commissioned to go tell others about this wonderful love of Jesus. The gift of mercy is not just for us, it's for everyone! To be set free from our past hurts and live a life victorious in Christ isn't a hidden secret we should keep to ourselves. We are to share it! Before Jesus ascended into heaven, He called His disciples together and ordained them for ministry. This means, with the assistance of the Holy Spirit, you are qualified to share the love of Jesus with anyone and everyone. Jesus told the disciples to go and make disciples of all nations; baptizing them in the name of God. When you handed your heart to the Lord, you became an equipped believer and are being commissioned to go and tell others how the Lord saved you. This is all for the expansion of the Kingdom of God. If you're feeling inadequate, be encouraged that the blood of Jesus qualifies you to spread the good news. You are the light! The light outshines the darkness (remember) and you are being called to be the light. Live as Jesus lived; love everyone, pray for them, heal the sick and cast out demons. Tell your redemptive story to others and model your life in a way that honors God.

Scriptures:
Matthew 28:16-20, Mark 16:14-20, Luke 24:47, 2 Corinthians 4:6

Reflective questions:
1. Do you fully understand your purpose?
2. What is God calling you to do?
3. Who is one person with whom you can share your story/testimony? Do you need to ask for boldness?

Foundations

Foundations

Congratulations! You did it! You hopefully have a better understanding of what I believe to be the 30 most important spiritual truths about Christianity. These foundational concepts will grow and change as you grow and change. Learning and growing into relationship with God involves taking a deeper dive into His word and opening the Bible. It involves knowing Him and making the effort to be closer to Him. I cannot express enough the importance of this relationship. To put God first allows His redemptive power to come alive in us and make us whole. God's intension was never to live separated from us. He loves us and so desperately wants to be reconciled back to us.

It's taken me a lot of years to truly grasp these concepts. I lived in fear not knowing that because God was with me, I could do anything! I never knew how to pray for people, to be full of thanksgiving or sing praises to God throughout my day. I never had intimacy with my heavenly Father. My worldly father dropped the ball on me so why would my heavenly Father be any different? This simply isn't true. These were negative things I carried around in my heart for many of my younger years. I truly am so grateful for the love God's shown me and how knowing these truths has healed my broken heart.

The scriptures are TRUE, they don't lie about who you are or how God feels about you. A lot of scriptures tell you one thing and then are followed by a result or promise. Fear not, God says for He is always with you (Isaiah 41:10)! If you follow His commandments, the number of your days will be long (Deuteronomy 4:40). He will prolong your life if you keep His words close to your heart. The result is spending eternity with God. I am IN, I don't know about you?

Foundations

My biggest hopes and dreams would be that each year (beginning of the year is always a good time) you would open this devotional and re-read it. I hope you will give it to your friend who believes in God but who doesn't do anything about it. As you grow spiritually, so will your faith, love and spiritual gifts. The meaning of these concepts will change and you will be able to see how your relationship with the Father has changed too. Is fear gone? Do you open your Bible more? Has your prayer life increased? The call, however, will always be the same; love God, love others and then go and do what Jesus did! Heal the sick, give to the poor and model a life for our Father in heaven.

Father God, you are so so good! You know what we need before we need it. You are relational and want to speak truth into our hearts. Lord, thank you for cleaning out the rubble and making room for joy, peace and love in our hearts. You are wonderful, mighty and the GREAT I AM! Your ways are above our ways and your love will reign forever. Lord I pray for everyone who read this book to be filled with the goodness of your love. I pray they will know you and then go and share your greatness with those around them. Thank you for using me to be a part of their journey. We praise your great and wonderful name and WE ALL SAY AMEN!!

Foundations

Thank you to my husband, Sean, who is loving, loyal and a Godly leader in our home. Thank you to my children who constantly show me love and a child-like faith in our heavenly Father. Thank you to Charity Creech and Angela Szymanski for your help with this devotional and cover.

Susan and family live in Bend, Oregon where they enjoy outdoor activities, the gym and family game nights full of love and laughter. They currently attend Epikos church where they enjoy weekly potlucks and a church family like no other.

www.ingramcontent.com/pod-product-compliance
Lightning Source LLC
Chambersburg PA
CBHW072018290426
44109CB00018B/2276